2009

God's Answer To 21st Century Terrorists

A How to Manual

Harvey K. McKelvey

Order this book online at www.trafford.com
or email orders@trafford.com

Most Trafford titles are also available at major online book retailers.

Printed in Victoria, BC, Canada.

ISBN: 978-1-4269-1772-1

Our mission is to efficiently provide the world's finest, most comprehensive book publishing service, enabling every author to experience success. To find out how to publish your book, your way, and have it available worldwide, visit us online at www.trafford.com

Trafford rev. 11/2/2009

 www.trafford.com

North America & international
toll-free: 1 888 232 4444 (USA & Canada)
phone: 250 383 6864 ✦ fax: 812 355 4082

Preview

Over the centuries terror has been used for many purposes, we would like to stress, that terror is used against Christians for various reasons. All terror is used to cause great fear and to intimidate God's people. In scripture there are many examples of terror. We will begin with Elisha. He is found in 2 Kings 6:8-23. This story of Elisha and the King of Syria starts with the King trying to intimidate, coerce, and cause fear in Elisha so that he would eventually do the Kings bidding. If he in fact did not he would be taken by the overwhelming force of the army. Did this form of terrorism work against Elisha? No! As God's people we are not supposed to be intimidated, or caused to fear regardless of the circumstance. Now I know there are examples of horrendous situations. However we are not to succumb to their statements of fear. To Elisha this army could have been as intimidating to the regular person as it was to the servant. Elisha spoke a word and the circumstance completely changed. Why was this? What gift of God was available to Elisha to change everything so that now Elisha was in control and caused them to bow at his feet? Elisha became the head and not the tail, the top not the bottom. Elisha spoke," Smite this people, I pray these with blindness." According to Elisha's word it was done. Did he also make the towns people blind? No of course not. Who were stricken then? Only the members ready to do Elisha harm. God is very selective. So what is a terrorist? It can be an army, arranged against you, literally or figuratively, you are, as the enemy thinks, supposed to be frightened to the point of surrendering.

Another story from the Bible, tells us about the man named Lot. He lived in a place called Sodom, I'm sure you remember the story. In this story the homosexual men of the city wanted to have the angels that had come to help Lot and his family. Now did the angels blind the men that came through the door? Yes they did. Were the citizens of Sodom blinded? No, only those determined to harm Lot and his guests. We see they had a change of mind when their sight was taken. What a wonderful gift, even for today.

Another story that is so misunderstood and not examined enough is the story about Paul (Saul). In fact in this story Paul was the terrorist in that century, killing Christians like Stephen and locking them in a prison. Jesus gave us this example so that we could use this against terrorists today. All the Christians were around and would not attempt to convert Saul, yet Saul had a zeal that others did not have. He had leadership as a gift. Many followed Saul. Then Jesus met him on the road to Damascus. While traveling on this road he was blinded by Jesus Himself. Saul's arrogance was halted. He was no longer a, Christian killing fanatic, but he soon knelt on his knees like a beggar and was willing to receive his instructions from God. Jesus then identified Himself to Saul and Saul was then instructed to go into Damascus into a certain place. Ananias, one of the strongest Christians of that time, was being terrorized by this man as were all other Christians. Ananias thought Jesus had made a mistake and didn't know who this Saul really was on the inside. Jesus then assured Ananias it was ok and he told him to lay hands on him so that he may receive his sight again, He then said that he would see a completely changed man. We need this in the 21st century. Why is this not in effect today?

Table of Contents

Chapter 1-What is a Terrorist?

Terror; Intense sharp overmastering fear a feeling of intense fear. When violence is used to maintain or achieve supremacy. Synonyms: Terror, horror, panic, fright, all imply extreme fear in the presence of danger or evil, an intense fear, which is prolonged. Horror implies a sense of shock at a danger which is also evil. Panic, is uncontrolled and unreasoning fear.

Terrorist; one who uses or favors terror methods, a political attempt, to demoralize a government with terror and fear, any group using terror to accomplish their goals.

Terrorize- to fill or overcome with terror to dominate, by intimidation.

Over the centuries terror has been used for many purposes, we would like to stress, that terror is used against Christian for various reasons. All terror is used to cause great fear and to intimidate God's people. In scripture there are many examples of terror. We will begin with Elisha. He is found in 2 Kings 6:8-23. This story of Elisha and the King of Syria starts with the king trying to intimidate, coerce, and cause fear in Elisha so that he would eventually do the Kings bidding. If he in fact did not he would be taken by the overwhelming force of the army. Did this form of terrorism work against Elisha? No! As God's people we are not supposed to be intimidated, or caused to fear regardless of the circumstance. Now I know there are examples of horrendous situations. However we are not to succumb to their statements of fear. To Elisha this army could have been as intimidating to the regular person as it was to the servant. Elisha spoke a word and the circumstance completely changed. Why was this? What gift of God was available to Elisha to change everything so that now Elisha was in control and caused them to bow at his feet? Elisha became the head and not the tail, the top not the bottom. Elisha spoke," Smite this people, I pray these with blindness." According to Elisha's word it was done. Did he also make the towns people blind? No of course not. Who were stricken then? Only the members ready to do Elisha harm. God is very selective. So what is a terrorist? IT can be an army, arranged against you, literally or figuratively, you are, as the enemy thinks, supposed to be frightened to the point of surrendering.

Another story from the Bible, tells us about the man named Lot. He lived in a place called Sodom, I'm sure you remember the story. In this story the homosexual men of the city wanted to have the angels that had come to help Lot and his family. Now did the angels blind the men that came through the door? Yes they did. Were the citizens of Sodom blinded? No, only those determined to harm Lot and his guests. We see they had a change of mind when their sight was taken. What a wonderful gift, even for today.

Another story that is so misunderstood and not examined enough is the story about Paul (Saul). In fact in this story Paul was the terrorist in that century, killing Christians like Stephen and locking them in a prison. Jesus gave us this example so that we could use this against terrorists today. All the Christians were around and would not attempt to convert Saul, yet Saul had a zeal that others did not have. He had leadership as a gift. Many followed Saul. Then Jesus met him on the road to Damascus. While traveling on this road he was blinded by Jesus Himself. Saul's arrogance was halted. He was no longer a, Christian killing fanatic, but he soon knelt on his knees like a beggar and was willing to receive his instructions from God. Jesus then identified Himself to Saul and Saul was then instructed to go into Damascus into a certain place. Ananias, one of the strongest Christians of that time, was being terrorized by this man as were all other Christians. Ananias thought Jesus had made a mistake and didn't know who this Saul really was on the inside. Jesus then assured Ananias it was ok and he told him to lay hands on him so that he may receive his sight again, He then said that he would see a completely changed man. We need this in the 21st century. Why is this not in effect today?

Do we have terrorists today? Yes we do. Can we identify them? Yes we can. Are there political and religious terrorists today? Yes there are. Where can we find them today? Over the world, and in every nation. Do we have terrorist on the mission field? Yes we do. What are some of their actions so we may identify them? They burn Churches and homes of Christians, they kill whole congregations, and they behead children going to and from school. They kill and imprison pastors and Christian leaders. What recourse do the Christians have? Until now they have been told to endure for God will avenge. But I say No, you have the power to stop this foolishness in its tracks. They can receive and believe the word, so that these terrorist become Christians just as Saul had became Paul and the Syrian army became friendly with Israel. This is a "believing God thing." Not a man thing.

In some nations of the world like in central Asia there are over 4 billion lost souls. The percentage of evangelical Christians among all of them is less than 5%. Jesus as we all know is coming soon, how are we to reach these before he comes? We need a new outlook, a new infusion of knowledge and wisdom, the old way is too slow and we will lose those that need to be saved if we do not change and allow God to work with us. Mark 16:20. Jesus and Christians, working together in spreading the Gospel, with signs and miracles happening among the, listeners, after the teaching. Blindness is a sign. Acts 2:7-47" praising God and having favor with all the people and the Lord added to the church daily such as should be saved".

For Christians then, a terrorist can be someone or many that want to stop you from witnessing. Stop your effectiveness, stop your winning the lost and kill you if need be.

Harvey K. McKelvey

For the Christian, a terrorist can be an attitude developed over time within us, which hinders our own witnessing, our soul winning, our prayer time and our relationship with Jesus and the Father and so we become cold or lukewarm (Rev 3:15-17). Here Jesus is talking to Christians or at least professing ones. Let us keep the terrorist inside, defeated and broken. We have enough trouble with the ones outside. So the terrorist operate on fear, causing untold trouble but we operate in love, perfect love casts out fear. 1 John 4: 17-21.

Chapter 2-How to Identify Them.

How they are identified. Matthew 7:16 "Ye shall know them by their fruits."

We want to know earlier than this, as pertaining to terrorists. We want to know before, not after the deed has been done.

I am reminded of the three young girls in India, coming home from school. When several young Muslim men attacked them, cutting off the heads of two of the girls and leaving the other badly scarred for life.

We would have liked to have known before hand, these were terrorist or be able to protect our children before this happened, but how? This is our question that will be answered in this book.

For many years I have witnessed the photos of Christian missionaries being killed and persecuted, I have heard untold testimonies of the same, ever since I was a small child. These stories and scenes always troubled me. In my unknowing way, I thought what a waste of blood, energy and the tools God provided for winning the lost. The churches burned down, homes burned and also bible schools. The local authorities would look the other was as if to say, "So what." That's what you get for coming to this country, to change us. Sometimes the local police are involved, sometimes the national army, sometimes the local youth, and sometimes it's the local religious community that feels threatened by their presence and they stir up trouble, using religion as a form of intimidation to get you to leave, and if not trouble will soon arise.

Now after 79 years of life, I still find it difficult to accept the horror and loss of life and property that comes to God's children, while working in these dangerous places. I'm focusing on the photo of the three young girls, two beheaded and one scarred for life. For some reason this photo really bothered my spirit, like no other. I found myself getting angry and kept saying, "There is something wrong with this picture. There is something wrong with this picture." This continued for a week or two. These Christians were here innocently doing the Lord's work, and their children are killed and scarred for life. This seemed not fair, something is terribly wrong with this picture. I was becoming righteously angry, thinking there must be a way for us as Christians to come against these onslaughts to our families and our work.

Then at 4am, about 2 weeks after my anger erupted, the Lord told me, "Paul, was a terrorist." This was mentioned three times, then silence. I began to ponder these words, and their meaning. I read and reread the account of Paul's conversion. Acts 9, The Holy Spirit said, "Do not read so quickly, check every second about what is taking place." So I did. I found that Paul wasn't blinded by the bright light, but by the gift of sight being removed from him by Jesus upon his arrival. I saw a "Red eyed fanatic." Saul was frothing at the mouth, because he hated these Christians so much and was acting like, a mad dog. No stopping him, his mind was made up and the chains were clanging as he approached Damascus. With every step he could see himself destroying and binding these Christians. "I'll show them, it's not healthy to worship this Jesus." Remember he had already consented to the death of Stephen. This man was not a loving person at all. He was as far away from love as a person could get.

Then Jesus came, "The bright light" indicated His presence. The gift of blindness was administered to Saul. Saul then fell to the ground. Once sight has been removed especially so suddenly, we feel we are safest on the ground. The only sight Saul had at this instant was the darkness of his own soul so dirty, black and filthy. Jesus then identified Saul's blindness to Himself. "Why are you persecuting me Saul? Who are you Lord? I am Jesus." Now Saul realizes God has come and he, Saul, has no excuse. All at once the red eyes were closed, the clanging of the chains ceased, the loud mouthed threats against God's children ceased. It's all so quiet, as Saul ponders his situation. Acts 9:6 "Trembling and astonished he asked, Lord what do you desire me to do?" See how quickly a terrorist will change for the good, once the blindness takes away the fury of their wicked heart they will then be just as strong for Jesus as they were for the devil, before conversion. Only more so now that they realize they are on the correct course in life. No more guessing just following.

May I expand a bit on what we have just learned? Thank you.

The focus of this book is upon the 4 billion Souls, in Asia, not reached, but to remain focused, I'll zero in on the 4 billion in Asia.

We have seen what a transformation occurred with Saul to Paul. Now we will be ministering to Buddhist, Muslims, Hindus, and to every other religion and sect in those regions. Some will become angry and try to do us harm, others will not, but we do not know who or when they will attack, so we will be prepared 24 hours every day. Our safety nets will be up and we will be ready to go to them and bring them into the kingdom. In fact you will be so excited about winning the Saul types, that the mellow ones will be a piece of cake. These terrorist types are the goal of this instruction, these will, when converted, be the strongest, the bravest, and the most bold of any Christian in this area. They will win their own, no matter which country. Our job is to prepare ourselves and our places of worship, schools, homes and each other especially the innocent children. Also do not forget to tell these new converts of this new evangelistic tool, for their own ministries. The Lord will be adding a great number of terrorist to your congregation. Be ready this is so new and exciting you can go anywhere on the earth and be a real soul winner for Jesus.

Chapter 3-Why does Jesus Love Them So Much?

John 3:16 tells us, "For God so loved the world, that He gave His only begotten Son, that whosoever believeth in Him should not perish but have everlasting life"

Jesus fulfilled the expression of the Father's love, by giving His life for us, all of us that now we have a pathway back to the father, which was destroyed, by sin, and we were all cast away from Him, as we all walked out of the Garden of Eden and out from His fellowship.

The terrorist as well as we, have a destiny, to fulfill the desires of the Father, in renewed fellowship. He wants to walk with us and talk with us, just like the days in the garden and the cool of the evening, the father would leave the throne room just to converse with His new creation and to walk with them.

The Father has never stopped desiring our fellowship and Jesus paid for our return by His life and His last words telling us to, "Go, into the whole world, and preach the gospel to every creature. He that believeth and is baptized shall be saved; but he that believeth not shall be damned." Mark 16:15-16

Now Jesus, knowing us in the flesh also, did not expect us to accomplish this task alone. So He made a suggestion or command in a demanding way. Acts 1:4-5, but wait don't try to do it on your own, "but wait for the promise of the Father, which, said He, ye have heard of me for John truly baptized with water, but ye shall be baptized with the Holy Ghost not many days hence." The disciples did not understand fully yet, like some of us, Jesus went on to say in Acts 1:8, "But ye shall receive power, after that the Holy Ghost is come upon you: and ye shall be witnesses unto me both in Jerusalem, and in all Judea, and in Samaria, and unto the uttermost parts of the earth."

Were the disciples empowered and ready before this? No and neither are we, until we complete the instructions to wait. Wait and be prepared for your Pentecost day. Acts 2:1-4, "and when this day of Pentecost was fully come, they were all with one accord in one place. And suddenly there came a sound from heaven as of a rushing mighty wind, and it filled the entire house where they were sitting. And there appeared unto them cloven tongues like as of fire, and it sat upon each of them. And they were all filled with the Holy Ghost, and began to speak with other tongues, as the Spirit gave them utterance."

Now that we have been baptized in the Holy Ghost, we have received power and authority, so that we may complete the admonition given in Mark 16:15-18. "Go ye into the entire world, and preach the gospel to every creature." Question, are terrorists creatures? Yes they are. We are not to preach only to the likeable and lovely but to the ugly and haters, the killers, the despots, the atheists, other religions which oppose themselves. Our job is very great and urgent in this time. Back to Mark 16:16 "He that believeth and is baptized shall be saved; but he that believeth not shall be damned. And these signs shall follow them that believe; (and are baptized in the Holy Ghost, like we are) in my name shall they cast out devils; they shall speak with new tongues, like we do. They shall take up serpents; and if they drink any deadly thing, it shall not hurt them; they shall lay hands on the sick, and they shall recover. Mark 16: 19-20, "So then after the Lord had spoken unto them, He was received up into heaven and sat on the right hand of God. And they went forth and preached everywhere, the Lord working with them, and confirming the word with signs following. Just like they did, we should be doing the same. Amen.

Why does, Jesus and the Father, love the terrorists so much? 2 Peter 3:9, "The Lord is not slack concerning His promise, as some men count slackness; but is longsuffering toward us, not willing that any should perish, but that all should come to repentance." This includes every false religion and the power these religions give to these terrorist, God loves them, and He wants you and me to love them, and do our best to win them. He promises to work with us to accomplish this task. He has equipped us with power and authority, all supernatural, also with superior wisdom and knowledge, to win those whom the Holy Spirit brings into our presence, and makes us aware of their need for Jesus in their lives.

In the following chapters, you will learn how God has instructed us to win even the most hate-filled terrorist and have them changed, like Saul, later Paul. Saul was a 1st century Christian terrorist, until Jesus showed us how to handle them, and not them handling us.

Chapter 4-Why should we love terrorist?

We begin this chapter with a series of questions, which will be answered later in the chapter.

1. Why should we love terrorist when they cut off the heads of our children as they are returning home from school.
2. Truly should we love terrorist when they attack our fellow believers, in their homes, in the church and while shopping. They burn our homes, our churches, and our meeting places. They threaten us with death if we do not leave their areas of influence,
3. Why should we love terrorist when they bear false witness against us in their courts of law. They lie about us and the Jesus we preach about. Saying we have blasphemed their prophet and elders?
4. Do these things bother you at all? What do you feel inside when you hear about these things? We are happy to know we are not there, experiencing these things.
5. How do you explain your actions after you hear about the persecution of Christians, World Wide? Is your spirit moved at all? Do you receive the admonition of the scripture, Hebrews 13:3 "Remember them that are in bonds, as bound with them; and them that suffer adversity as being yourselves also in the body"?
6. How can Christians perform well when fear has gripped their hearts, as they wait for another onslaught from the enemy? We pray for them, yes. We ask God's protections over them, yes. But when the missionaries and workers in these regions do not know how to protect, themselves, for they were not taught the things that you are learning.

Then they are open game, for the enemy to crush, destroy, belittle and intimidate these followers of Jesus. 1 John 4:17-21 "Perfect love casts out fear. So we are being changed into a fearful being, not the strong man or woman or child that God has equipped with His armor, shield etc. So we are fearful because of a lack of knowledge." Hosea 4:6 "My people are destroyed for a lack of knowledge

7. So we should love the terrorists because God does, and He commands us to love our enemies. Also He isn't willing that any should perish, 2 Peter 3:9 "... Not willing that any should perish, but that all should come to repentance."

8. Then by allowing fear to permeate our being, and acting accordingly we are sinning unconsciously, because God has provided weapons for our use, and we did not know they existed. As a consequence many, many Christians have been murdered, churches burned, and untold millions of dollars wasted, because of this lack of understanding. Plus try to imagine, all the so called terrorists that have been condemned to hell, because we lacked the proper understanding.

9. I would like to make one more observation. Saul was a leader and His zeal for God placed him in an authoritative position. He had more zeal than any of his followers, so he became the leader. Now how many of the terrorists, past and present, are also strong leaders? Have we been letting strong leaders perish, because we are afraid of them? As was the Damascus Christians. They absolutely wanted nothing to do with Saul. Yet Jesus chose a leader, a strong leader.

10. What would a strong leader of the terrorists be, if converted? Another Paul? So let us understand, "Like Jesus did," The value of these strong leaders, convert them and like Paul, they will be the strongest and most sincere of all our converts. The secret, do not be afraid and use the blind tools to convert them.

Chapter 5-What Do the Terrorists Have That We Have Missed?

1. I briefly mentioned this at the end of chapter 4. We want the terrorist leaders the rest will follow their lead. We want the worst of them because God has a plan for their life just like Saul. These leaders are usually the most educated, the most trusted, and the most feared because they are brutal in their conduct, and will use every means at their disposal to keep the followers in line. We want them. We want them because they know their cultures and the traditions of the areas. They know their countrymen and what will most influence them.

2. Once converted these leaders and their followers, will provide the strong leadership, required of the Evangelists, for this end time revival.

3. In the Asia area there are over 4 billion people that have not heard the Gospel. Jesus is coming very soon, as we all know. If we do not make a greater effort to win these people, then how will we feel, when we are in heaven getting ready to receive our reward, and have Jesus pat us on the back and say, "Well done my good and faithful Christian enter into, the joy of the, Lord." Then before He lets us go He will show us a picture of the Earth and point to this area where 2/3 of the population of the world lives, then ask us "Oh by the way, what have you done to save these 4 billion souls headed for an eternity in hell? Have you prayed for them? Have you been concerned enough to lay awake at night, asking me for wisdom and knowledge as to how you can be more effective? Or have

you decided it's not your problem, and for those remaining that have not heard, the 144,000 Jewish Evangelist can win during the tribulation? "I do not know about you, but I would be so ashamed my head would be lowered, my heart broken, because I would realize as much as I accomplished in this life, so much more could have been done, if only I had known God's perspective, pursued it and not so many of my own desires.

4. My heart is saddened today as I write, realizing that many Christians before us, have gone home to be with the Lord. Leaving this task for us to accomplish. They did not know many of the things we know now, especially in the 21st century things are changing. Evil is more mature. Have you seen it? However my concern is that righteousness should be more mature also, since the word declares that in Isaiah 59:19 "When the enemy shall come in like a flood, the spirit of the Lord shall lift up a standard against him." So today in the 21st century, the Holy Spirit is revealing how to use the weapons of our warfare more effectively. This one weapon of blindness has been with us since the beginning, now we need this weapon for Evangelism, more than at anytime in our history. We must win the lost at any cost. We will quench the fiery darts of the enemy. Save, baptize and teach these former enemies, to be Gospel warriors for Jesus Christ.

When these terrorist are caught by the authorities, we find most are very well educated; they are not a bunch of nobodies. They have degrees, Doctorates, MBA's, and Bachelor degrees. These people are smarter than the average person on the street. They are more intelligent than the average person. So why do they embrace the terrorist ways? They need Jesus and do not know it. God wants them in His work because once they know the right way, their zeal and enthusiasm, will be brought to the new field of endeavors just like the apostle Paul.

Chapter 6-Have They Been Calling Us?

1. Many years ago I was working with young boys. Not having experience, other than my own sons I found a psychology book on how to teach and influence children especially boys. One article, I remember, had to do with the actions of boys. When they wanted your attention one of the ways they get your attention is to be the meanest little boy in the group, this way you will think he is a little devil, but if you single him out and begin to befriend him, he will totally change and you will be so surprised and blessed.

    I have recently thought about this method when reading about Saul and his conversion. He seemed to be the meanest man the Christians had ever seen. Even having Stephen killed and going after all the rest of them, until even Ananias thought of him as a terrorist. All the church was in hiding from this man and his helpers. The Christians of that day would absolutely have nothing to do with this man. Yet, Jesus knew the psychology of this man and when Saul was arrested and lost his eyesight, he became more manageable and willing to learn. Jesus then described to him, his error and introduced Himself to Saul. Saul then called Him "Lord my new leader and my God." Jesus gave us the example as to how to treat a terrorist. One that is well educated, full of arrogance, and full of self worth, a leader of the men who followed him blindly.

2. First we must be prepared to deal with their blindness, since they will want to receive instruction, now that their

sight is gone. They may want to argue and rant for a while, but when they see their fussing is getting them nowhere, they will begin to receive your message of salvation.

"We must remember at all times we are not the ones that have arrested these men and women." It's Jesus and they are to be introduced to Him first, before anything else happens. Remember the Holy Spirit is working with you, to bring these to salvation and your church will be added to daily. Just as the scripture says, take your cue from Paul's conversion in small steps then you will understand.

3. Now we have no shortage of terrorists to work with. They are all over the world. So you can begin looking wherever you are. Try to identify them. Set up your perimeter and wait, but be fully prepared for the occasion when it happens. The rest of the terrorist will begin to fear God's people and will try to stay away, until they think they have an advantage over you then they will strike. However we are prepared at all times, 24/7 to meet their needs.

4. Since the first century terrorist was arrested, Saul, there have been millions of their kind throughout the Earth. At this time I am thinking about all the Muslim, Hindu, Buddhist and others which deny Jesus and persecute the Christians. I'm reminded of the three girls in India where just recently two were beheaded and the 3rd very badly scarred for life. Had these girls been prepared with a blindness perimeter this could have had a different ending. These terrorist are telling us something "We are in need of your Jesus, can you hear us?" "We are caught up in our sin and false religion, can you set us free?" "Can you help provide an encounter with your Jesus, just as the apostle Paul had?"

5. They are calling us, do you hear them? Do I? Will we pray and prepare our hearts and minds to this new concept, to win more and more of the lost to Jesus Christ, so that when He points to the 4 billion people area on the earth,

we can gladly say with rejoicing "With your leadership Jesus, yes, we were very much involved and to the Holy Spirit we were winners, not losers. We made every effort to win all of them. Thank you again Jesus for the new tools and the knowledge in how to use them. Thank you also precious Holy Spirit for the power and authority you have given, you make this Christian life so exciting and rewarding."

Chapter 7-Now What Do We Do? Prepare For Battle.

1. Let us be refreshed as to what we have learned so far about terrorist and God's plan for their salvation.

    a. In Chapter 1, we decided what a terrorist was.
    b. Chapter 2, described how to identify them.
    c. Chapter 3, the great question, why does Jesus love them so much?
    d. Chapter 4, why should we love them when they have caused so much trouble?
    e. Chapter 5, what do these terrorist have that we have missed?
    f. Chapter 6, have they been calling us by their actions?
    g. Chapter 7, now what do we do?

2. What I am about to reveal is absolutely essential for anyone involved in or active in any Christian work or endeavor, with for and among any terrorist group secular or religious. You must know these things as an individual; teach it to your friends, every one of them, your children, all of them, regardless of age. We have to tell the members in your fellowship, church, synagogue or any place of Christian worship. Because your lives will depend upon this information, your physical life.

3. The remainder of this little "How to" book will cover all the necessary requirements for being a successful terrorist warrior.

    The first thing every Christian should know is how to lead a person to Christ, if you do not know, nor care to learn, then this warfare is not for you and we do not want you in our ranks. Just stay home and be a nice little Christian. Later in the book there will be instruction for introducing a terrorist to Jesus. Again this is the first step in preparation to be a terrorist warrior. Your life and mine will be dependent upon this ability and capability.

Let me illustrate what I mean and the seriousness of this decision. Many years ago I was a member of an Evangelistic church. Shortly after joining this church, I became aware that the people had a different idea about how to introduce someone to Jesus. Some had an idea how, but not very practical. Others absolutely knew nothing, thinking this was the pastor's duty, not theirs. I approached the pastor after one of our meetings and asked him if he would consider some basic classes in salvation, and teaching the congregation what was required scripturally, for a person to be saved so that the entire congregation knew and would be saying the same thing, when instructing someone for salvation. This pastor totally shocked me when he said, "As long as I am pastor of this church we will not ever do such a thing." I realized I was attending the wrong church so I and my family left the following Sunday afternoon, after bringing in all the papers for the church. I never returned. Since then I have found this information to be most helpful and absolutely essential for salvation.

Now in this terrorist ministry you will begin to see how this works into your life and ministry. So once again I emphasize strongly, learn how to lead a person to Jesus and make sure every member of your team knows this basic information also. It's vital! "Roman way"

4. Self preparation:

Take time alone with the Father with Jesus and the precious Holy Spirit. A lot of time, because we will need to know what the Holy Spirit wants us to do and how to do it. So we must have a very personal relationship with the, "God Head".

We must be baptized with the Holy Spirit, with the evidence of speaking in other tongues. We all need this so that the other gifts of the spirit may work in and through us. Jesus said in Luke 24:49, "And behold, I send the promise of my Father upon you but tarry ye in the city of Jerusalem, until ye be endued with power from on high." Then in Acts 2:4 we find the disciples being baptized with the Holy Spirit, then they went out preaching everywhere. So we need followers of Jesus that know the word, act the word and do the word to the approval of God almighty, then exploits can be accomplished by Him, working through us as guided vessels.

5. These followers of Jesus will be very closely knit units. "No showoffs, no cowboys," but a dedicated group with the salvation of 4 billion people as their task and purpose. Now there will be many native workers that will need to be taught this way and shown how it works, so they can go and start fellowships, churches, Bible schools and what ever the Lord wants He gets. These natives may go from country to country, teaching, showing and telling in the Bible schools and churches of that land, what they have learned and in just a short time a revival will be happening, just before Jesus returns, so let us be working in the harvest when He comes.

6. Many of us have been taught over the years how to apply anointing oil over our door posts and rooms of the house for protection. We also anoint with oil those who are sick. But in our terror battles we are going to use the anointing idea in a new way, which will bring terrorist and unbelievers, into our fellowship and we shall grow greatly, as God brings those daily who need to be saved. More on this later.

Chapter 8: Prepare The Playing Field!

I love athletics, especially football. So I will illustrate my thoughts through the combat of football and the opposing teams. In our case we are not of this world John 15:19 but we are in combat with forces of this world. The goal is not a touchdown but the winning of another soul to Christ.

The forces arranged against us are spiritual and of this world, unrepentant sinners and satanic forces. We, on the other hand, are not of this World, but are trying to win these lost ones to Jesus before they perish. The results are life or death situations, therefore the preparations for this battle must be strict, intense and very dedicated. Our success depends upon it. Possibly even our lives.

Now let us take a peek into an actual combat situation and see from the sidelines what is happening. Are we winning or losing? Can we improve our effectiveness?

Testimonies, illustrations, of the 3 girls in India two beheaded and I escaped with scars for life.

In these days and for far too long, Christians are being killed needlessly because this level of evangelism has not been taught or understood. However, in these last days, as the enemy comes in like a flood the Lord will raise a standard against him. In these days, terrorism is spreading all over the World. We may be relatively safe today but it's coming to our country and every country of the world. So now is the time to prepare everyone. No one excluded unless you desire to be unprotected.

This is the standard of evangelization that is raised, against the enemies of Jesus Christ and He wants you to be a part of this great movement as He demonstrates His power, on behalf of the Christians, for the ingathering of souls in these last days.

I like to think of this plan as a, Godly trap, an invisible trap. 1. Used for Saul of Tarsus, by Jesus. 2. Used against the homosexuals of Sodom, by the angels. 3. Used against the Syrian Army, by Elisha. 4. Now Jesus is preparing us for the use of this invisible trap against the terrorists of every nation and religion, which is against the gospel of Jesus Christ and He wants us to be taught this new and extreme method in evangelism. We must know what to do and how to do it, for their well being and ours, for the safety of everyone and everything under their authority.

As a small child, this protection is for you.

As a student, at home or at school or in between, this protection is for you.

As a shopper going to the market, this protection is for you

As Christian, gathering in a home or church for services, this is for you, as a Christian in street ministry, as a Christian in door to door ministry, as a Christian in Bible school, high school, elementary and kindergarten. Stay prepared, we are coming into perilous times.

We need you on the front lines winning the lost, not in a grave, where your usefulness has then ceased to be effective in evangelism.

So let us all pray together, protect each other, teach and cover for each other and make sure the trap has been placed around everyone you hold dear. As a believer cover your family members, so that even in our church services, which may be interrupted by the cry of the blind, outside the church building. We must be prepared to go at once to them. Identify their blindness with the presence of Jesus, to forgive them, to save them and totally change them. Then, like the Apostle Paul, their sight will be restored and they will be new creatures in Jesus Christ, taking the fury of their hatred for Jesus and us, now changed, to love and win all their countrymen and fellow unbelievers.

This new evangelism must be taught here at home the U.S.A, and to every Christian throughout the Earth.

Missionaries in hostile lands are being murdered, maimed, destroyed and discouraged because they do not know. We must take this powerful information to them. They must not only know this information, but practice it, 24 hours every day. This is a higher calling, a more serious and effective calling, for these troubling times.

Now you may think this will not apply to you because you are in the U.S.A, England or some other country where the gospel can be preached without problems. But my dear Christian friends, we are in the last days and these, so-called Christian Nations are going to experience terrorism in the same way as our brothers and sisters in China, India, Afghanistan, Laos, Cambodia, and Vietnam. So please, heed the calling to prepare yourselves for this new harvest of souls. Be a victor not a victim.

All the methods for evangelism which we have been taught for years and have used in the past are still relevant. This new way is to prepare you for the conversion of the radicals and terrorist which you will be encountering in the near future, without fear or trembling. My people are destroyed for a lack of knowledge. Well now you are being equipped with knowledge, before the trouble arrives.

"God the Father," "God the Son" and "God the Holy Spirit" wants you to stand your ground and advance before the enemy, not retreat. They want you to be alive well and excited about the position you are in, the knowledge you have and the love you are about to share. They are ready to work with you if you will stand without fear because perfect love casts out fear. God wants you to grow, where you are.

I want you the reader and every Christian friend to look at these radical and terrorist people in another way. You should be aware that they are the crème of the devil's followers. They have taken their oath of allegiance to him and have proven themselves, by the killing and destroying of God's children and

God's property. Now, just like Saul, the terrorist, became Paul the Apostle. Now our terrorist will become front line powerful evangelist in these times just like Paul. These folk will turn the tide and win thousands in their own nations, for the greatest harvest of all times.

In closing this chapter, I want to let you in on a heavenly view of our planet.

Now if you would take a compass. Set the pointer at the northern tip of Burma. Then find the 100 mile mark and draw a circle. Then every 100 miles draw an outer circle out to 1000 miles in all directions. You will be looking at a "Bulls eye target" Now within this 1000 mile, area there are 4 billion souls that have not been evangelized as yet. There are only 5% Christians in this area. Now after 2008 years we have not made much of a dent in this population, yet we all know Jesus is coming soon. Will you be satisfied to have Jesus welcome you into the Kingdom of God by saying "Well done, my good and faithful servant," then He would ask you "Oh, by the way" as He points to this "Bulls eye target," and then asks you "Were you concerned that these 4 billion souls were not evangelized? Did you pray at all about them? Or did you leave it up to others? Did you help them in any way?" Would you feel guilty?

Well maybe, if you were not trying to learn how to use these new evangelistic tools. Once you learn these techniques, you can then answer "Yes sir" and feel not guilty at all because you were prepared for the task and volunteered for service in giving, through prayer, or actually going to these places.

Chapter 9: We Must Be Prepared For Them. "The fruit of the righteous is a tree of life and whoever captures souls is wise." Proverbs 11:30.

From the oldest to the youngest among us we must be prepared to receive these terrorist into our midst. Much of the teaching will take place in churches and bible studies, so the studies must be pertinent to the salvation message, to prepare them for deeper studies as they progress.

Now while the Bible studies are very important for their growth. The most crucial moment for them and for us is the initial contact with them. Remember Jesus has just blinded them and now it's our duty to help them identify their blindness, with the arrest by Jesus Christ. Not Mohammed or some other man of god. Remember Proverbs 1:7 "The fear of the Lord is the beginning of wisdom." These have just had their first encounter with God. The Lord and fear has settled in their hearts, "beginning of wisdom." Now we can explain to them Jesus and His requirements for the rest of their lives. Always remember the steps to follow. 1. First they are blinded like Saul. 2. Next we must introduce them to Jesus. 3. Like Saul, they will ask what I must do. At this point their hatreds have vanished and they are ready to listen. 4. Now we can give the salvation message for them to accept or reject. 5. If they accept then we can make plans for inside ministering after you make sure they are not armed or carrying a bomb vest. 6. Those not wanting to accept but want to reject, then after a bit more persuasion they still object, then turn them around and tell them the proper direction to go to get home, or to their village. Now at this point I do not know if their sight will be restored or not I suspect not. But those coming in for more instruction will have their sight restored shortly. Paul was blind for 3 days as Ananias counseled with him.

So as I mentioned earlier, this first encounter with them can be a bit scary for they will be armed with guns such as RPG's, machetes, knives and etc. But do not be fearful or afraid. Remember blindness disarmed the Syrian army. Blindness disarmed Saul and company; blindness disarmed the homosexuals at Sodom and Gomorrah. So this will be no different. Remember God is doing, His part, so that you have the opportunity to do yours. In Acts 2:47 "God adding to your fellowship daily those that are to be saved." This means to become perfect in our relation to God and these new people, so that God can continue to add to us daily. Isn't this exciting?

Instructions to lead a person to Christ:

1. Now with these blind men and women coming into our fellowship, it will require a different response from us. The terrorists will need to be fed and given a place to sleep for a while, during their instruction. Someone will be required to be with them for protection and council around the clock 24/7.

2. Every Christian from the youngest to the oldest in our fellowship must be familiar with, how to lead a person to Jesus and what is required: I personally like the, "Roman way," it is easier to remember even for the very young. This requirement will be more apparent as we continue. The roman way is shown in Romans 3:23, Romans 6:23, Romans 5:8, Romans 10:9-10, and Revelations 3:20. When the terrorist understand these verses and embrace them, as the response Jesus wants from them, then they will be saved.

3. Once the instructions is complete and these new Christians are walking with Jesus, then I would recommend a baptism service in which they may be baptized in water and the Holy Spirit, after which hands may be laid upon them for the recovery of their sight. Get ready for the most exciting praise and worship you have ever heard, for these are and will be so overjoyed and excited in their new future now with Jesus Christ. They will be fully persuaded as was the apostle Paul, that now nothing can separate them from God's love.

Chapter 10: The Standard Has Been Raised.

Hosea 4:6 "My people are destroyed for a lack of knowledge."

"When the enemy shall come in like a flood the spirit of the Lord will lift up a standard against him and put him to flight for He will come like a rushing stream which the breath of the Lord drives. Isaiah, 59:19 Amp," "Arise from the depression and prostration in which circumstances have kept you; rise to a new life! Shine and be radiant with the glory of the Lord; for your light is come and the glory of the Lord is risen upon you!" Isaiah, 60:1, "For behold darkness shall cover the earth and dense darkness all peoples; but the Lord shall arise upon you and His glory shall be seen on you." Isaiah 60:2.

We have in recent years seen the rise of the Muslim terrorist, the Hindu, Buddhist and many others. This is the time to let our light shine, take Jesus into these camps of festering hatred and with Him, win the worst of the worst, that these may also fill their spiritual fruit basket with souls of their own people, and others as the Lord leads them. Truly the enemy is coming in like a flood and the Lord has raised the new standard against this onslaught to the peoples of the earth. Since evil is maturing more and more each year, we will be encountering these situations more and more. Even in America, so get ready, do not be destroyed for lack of knowledge, arm yourself and your loved ones with God's plan of counter attack with love for these so called terrorist which really are, tough, Christians, only they do not know it yet.

There are two classes of people and a different approach is needed for each. Recently I attended an intercessors conference, which spoke of spiritual warfare and the need to rescue the lost. The message was wonderful, but afterward the word rescue seemed to be too soft an approach to what was happening in my spirit. I began to pray about this and soon the Lord answered me this way. We are having an evangelistic service in a terror infested part of the world. The service begins inside a building, the message had been given and several persons were seeking salvation at the altar, when all of a sudden a cry was heard that 40 terrorist had arrived at the compound. They were threatening to burn the building and if anyone tried to flee they would be killed. Now these terrorist also need the Lord as much as the seekers at the altar. The ones at the altar are being rescued while the terrorist need to be arrested, as was Saul of Tarsus. However, the services were conducted in such a way that the rescue was available but the arrest was absent.

Now with this picture in our mind we should have also provided the arrest ministry. This could be done by the leaders, pastors, evangelist, deacons and the church helpers. They would march single file around the building only about 100ft. to 100yds. From it, providing a perimeter of faith around the building, saying and invoking God's help in the services by pronouncing, anyone coming to do us evil, will be blinded as they cross this invisible fence. Now if and when the terrorist arrive they will be blinded, arrested. Now you can have some of your church workers, deacons, pastors, evangelist, also go outside the Church meeting, to rescue those that have just been, "arrested". Rescue for the mild and respectful ones, arrest for the rowdy killers until they become servants of the, Most High GOD.

We have just spared many souls from being killed in the line of duty. They will live to continue this ministry for years to come. Remember your physical usefulness is not a factor when you are in the grave, you can no longer help. So do not be a victim but a victor, taking all the knowledge God has given you to both kinds of people. The church will grow much faster, the faith level much higher, the commitment to God's ways much more lasting and enduring as you rejoice with these new, Paul's, Peter's, and John's.

So we see God has truly raised a standard against the evil that lurks in the world. It will no longer be evangelistic services as usual. We must prepare the outside as well as the inside of our meeting places, our homes, our churches, and even every individual in the home. Be sure a 5 foot invisible fence is established around your children as they go to and from school, around mother and father, around everyone you care about, and know that when someone is blinded in your presence you must identify this blindness to Jesus Christ, and their rejection of His love, then they will be more willing to hear you.

Now you can understand why every Christian must know how to lead someone to Jesus Christ. It is most important; these may be blinded many miles from a church, school or home. Maybe while you are boating or mountain climbing, it can happen anytime and it's your responsibility, to get this person saved and into a fellowship, so that later their sight may be restored.

Yes the standard is raised for the sinner and for us also, for we are required to be more sensitive to the things of God, for our own lives depend upon it. God is adding to our church daily. In acts 2:47 it says "those who were being saved from spiritual death."

For the terrorist that are being saved, we must provide a place for sleeping and food for a few days until their sight is restored. This is another thing we have not been concerned with up until now, so we must be ready to do more, than has been our custom. We will be personally involved and be personally accountable for these blinded ones. So our mission has become greater in these last days. The regular folks, we have become accustomed to, and the new terrorist folk, that need special care.

I am so excited about being in on God's end time harvest and helping it get started.

Chapter 11- The End Times Are Upon Us.

The focus of this chapter as many of the previous ones will be on the 4 billion lost persons in the most densely populated areas of the Earth.

We all know that the time is critical for the return of Jesus, will be very soon. According to Ezekiel, 38:1-6, it says; Russia, Iran, Ethiopia, Libya, and others will soon be attacking Israel. For centuries Russian and Iran have never had national dealings, however within the last few years, Iran and Russia are becoming very cozy with each other, with nuclear reactors and the like, arms, missiles and etc. Russia will be the, big dog, to lead the Islamic Countries against Israel. So watch them closely.

With this warning in mind we continue to prepare for the abundant harvest, which has been promised in Matthew 9:37-38 and John 4:35. We must be praying to the Lord of harvest to send workers into the fields. The information in this book will help in producing more laborers for this end time harvest. We must be diligent and obey the Holy Spirits call, to join ourselves in this endeavor.

Now since so many are yet to be reached one would think, to volunteer, would be a real treat to be working with the Lord every day. How exciting! But this is not the case. We read in Isaiah 59:15b-16a "And the Lord saw it and it displeased Him that there was no justice and He saw that there was no man, and wondered that there was no intercessor no one to care for these lost souls, allowing them to go into eternity lost and forsaken."

I am reminded about the Garden of Eden where the Lord came walking in the cool of the day to visit with His new creations, Adam and Eve. Even though God was surrounded with all the splendor and majesty of the throne room, with all the worship and adoration, but still there was something missing. God wanted to fellowship with His new human creation, to talk to them to ask how they were doing and if they were happy in their new environment. He wanted to hear from them, as well as to instruct them.

Now let us fast forward to the 21ˢᵗ century. Since God never changes, then He still delights in listening to us here on this planet, but what must He be thinking, when He visits the far east and sees so many unsaved souls and so few people interested in finding them, winning them and preparing them for eternity. As He walks in these areas alone, it says in Isaiah 59:16 "He looked for a man or woman that would care enough about these lost ones to intervene in their behalf before the Lord." He just wanted 1 man or woman. Do you care about the lost? Would you be willing to join others in praying for these? Would you be willing to go to these areas for ministry?

Years ago, God had pronounced to the Israelites that because of sin and rebellion He was preparing to disperse them to the four quarters of the Earth, but before He did, He looked for a man that would intercede like Moses, someone who cared enough about their country and the people, to ask the Lord for more time for a chance to talk to them. But He found no one. So they were scattered throughout the earth, as they are to this day.

Now in the 21ˢᵗ century can you imagine God walking among the Hindu's, Buddhist's and Muslims plus many more tribes and people and finding no one to pray for them, no one to care for them because of fear of the terrorist. Well I have news for you; God has given us the antibiotic for terrorism, no more fears, no more anxiety, but with a heart for the lost and with the power of the Holy Spirit, we can go forth boldly to declare the love of Jesus to these lost and hurting souls, with the knowledge to win them for Jesus. "The Lord working with us", is adding to the church daily those that are to be saved. Acts 2:47, terrorist and the more mellow souls to Jesus, they are both lost and we have been commissioned to find them and win them.

When "God the Father", "God the Son", and "God the Holy Spirit" leaves the throne room to walk in your neighborhood to talk to you, are you ready to talk about important things, like eternity, winning the lost, worship and prayer time, or are you most interested in the kids not minding, the car that is getting old, the gossiping neighbors, or even the time required to prepare food or go shopping. My dear friend He will listen to your complaints, and quietly slip away, to look for fellowship of a spiritual nature, the things that Jesus came to fulfill. Remember, God is not willing that any should perish, but that all should turn to repentance 2 Peter 3:9b. We need His view of the world to guide us and His word to sustain and empower us to a better relationship.

Have you ever thought about the relationship that Enoch and God had? Their fellowship was so intimate and intense that they walked back into heaven, for God wanted and desired his fellowship so much, this also happened with Elijah. Why am I bringing this up? It's because the next time God comes walking into your dreams or thoughts, quickly take His hand and do not let Him walk away without you. He came to fellowship, please do not disappoint Him. Instead enjoy Him, love Him, worship Him, talk to Him, praise Him, and believe Him. Never, no never let Him walk away alone. Place your hand in His and walk forever, never let go. Use the best language you can master when talking to Him, show respect. He has come to hear your voice, make Him happy to have come to see you. I know you will be happy to be in His presence. Please know He sees you as a saint, in snow white clothes, not a dirty old sinner. His son's blood has cleansed you, forgive you and now you can fellowship with the Father on a 1 to 1 basis, because of Jesus.

So listen to Him, He will tell you what you must do to be a part of this end time harvest, for terrorist and the mellow fellow, we want all of them and are willing to go to them, sacrifice to be there, and win them in the mighty name of Jesus.

Chapter 12-Get Right, Stay Right, and Be Holy.

Several years ago at a Bible study meeting the question of a small white lie was discussed. Many believed a small white lie would go unchallenged by the Holy Spirit. However, a few days after this discussion I was praying and asked the Holy Spirit to reveal how a little white lie looked in His eyes. This is what happened. I was standing in an open space and someone was standing next to me, on the right side. As I was watching this person, a very beautiful white robe was placed around this person. I examined the robe and the texture of it was like velvet, the depth of the material was so very deep and so exceptional was the whiteness of the cloth. After examining the material, which must be at least 2 to 3 million dollar material, so expensive and beautiful, I noticed movement on my left like someone was walking to an open topped bucket about the size of a 5 gallon pail with a handle. In the bucket was a substance like old used oil from vehicles, nearly full. The person began to pick up this bucket and I knew immediately what they were going to do and I began to scream, "No! No! No! Don't do it." But the person acted like they couldn't hear me, or was disregarding my pleas altogether. The bucket was picked up and the person moved toward the other person on my right and threw the dirty oil onto the beautiful white garment, causing the front of the garment to be dirty and oil soaked. I wept bitterly for several days, yet even now, I become ill whenever I see this episode. The Lord reminded me, "This is what a little white lie, looks like to me, whenever you tell them you and your study group thinks its ok and I will overlook such a lie as being insignificant." "How could I when your sin is so obvious." He then asked me a question, "Do you think you will be happy with all the other saints clothed in pure white, and you with this on your robe?"

The first part of this chapter is Get right. That means ask for and receive forgiveness for all the lies, small and great, and any other sins you have been committing, stop it. Repent, that your righteous garment will again show your right relationship with Jesus Christ.

The last chapter was about the end times being upon us, which is very true. Please dear saint of the Living God do not be caught with soiled and dirty garments. This is an indication of a dirty, unforgiving, heart. The Holy Spirit has shown you how you look to Him in these filthy clothes, so clean up and be ready, then read the second part of this 3 part chapter.

Stay Right.

Now that we know what even small sins look like to God I want to encourage you again to get right with the Lord because time is of the essence. I would also like to tell you do not procrastinate. Get right or you may be left and become one of the sorriest people on the earth. One other admonition is necessary. Galatians 6:7-8. Be not deceived "God is not mocked for whatsoever a man sows, that shall he shall also reap. For he that sows, to his flesh shall of the flesh reap corruption; but he that sows to the spirit shall of the spirit reap life everlasting."

So, to stay right repent often, accept forgiveness, and become a good disciple over your body, for you are in charge of it. Do not let, disrespectful and vulgar vocabulary proceed, out of your mouth. Do not use the Lord's name in vain, for these things also tarnish your righteous robe. Do not mock God, but be honest, upright respectful and worship Him. Protect your precious gift, of righteousness. This reminds me of a chorus we learned many years ago. "I gave Him my old tattered garments; He gave me a robe of pure white; now I'm feasting on mama from heaven and that's why I'm happy tonight."

Find other Christians to hang out with, so that you may share with each other the joys and hurts you suffer, so that they may pray for you and you pray for them, until that wonderful day arrives when we shall see Him, face to face.

While you are learning to disciple yourself, you are growing stronger and stronger so that soon you will be used in the battle for the terrorist of which this book is about. I am sure you understand, that anyone weak in the faith can not be victorious, in winning these people to Jesus. In these last days God is looking for, red hot warriors, not cold, not lukewarm ones as written in Revelations 3 15-16 "I know thy works that thou art neither cold nor hot: I would thou were cold or hot. So then because thou art lukewarm and neither, cold or hot, I will spew thee out of my mouth." Revelations 3:11 "Behold, I come quickly; hold that fast which thou hast, that no man take thy crown."

This is the most exciting time in history to be alive. Time as we know it is drawing to a close. There is still so much to do before Jesus comes. The Holy Spirit is enlisting and developing people to join His might army, for the closing days before His return. Do you hear the call, to give Him all your strength, your mind, and your will? He is calling us to be victors not victims. The choice is ours. Please join me, for I have chosen the plan of the victors, and I wish for you to do the same. Together let us close out this age with the shouts of victory, with great joy, peace, power and praise for our God and Jesus Christ. The one that loved us so much that He gave Himself for us that we might live, let us now give ourselves to Him.

Be Holy.

1 Peter 1:15-16 "But as He which hath called you is holy, so be ye holy in all manner of conversation, because it is written

be ye holy; for I am Holy sacred, pure, blameless, consecrated, Holy."

Ephesians 1:4 "Even as He chose us, actually picked us out for Himself, as His own in Christ before the foundation of the world; that we should be holy and blameless in His sight, even above reproach before Him in love.

Dear church leaders, pastors, evangelist, teachers, deacons, prophets and everyone attending church as members or visitors. Please, please treat others in love, respect, honesty and truth for as you teach and become leaders of men and women, boys and girls you are being faithful to Jesus and the Hoy Spirit who is concerned with our progress in truth.

I am reminding you of these truths, to bring the emphasis to the new terrorist converts that you will be training and teaching. These men, women and children are like a race horse, trained to win at any cost. These front line troops of Satan are now the energetic force, for evangelism in the army of Jesus Christ. They have been redeemed from death and know their mission now in life, is the true mission with a heavenly goal, which they will embrace with all their being. Also since they will feel in their spirits that they are late comers, to the Lord Jesus Christ, His coming is very soon and they will want to make up for lost time, by being super sensitive to the Holy Spirit's calling and direction. They will want to save everyone they meet. Their joy and respect will be so great for Jesus, that they will not want to sleep because time will be wasted, or so they think. Their speed will be 100% full throttle all the time.

So we, as leaders and teachers of these new race horses for Jesus, must teach them properly so that they will not be ashamed of the teaching they received nor of knowing Jesus at any time in their life, but be like the apostle Paul fervent and with one goal, one view, straight ahead for Christ Jesus. Their dedication and honesty will affect many, as they come in contact with these racing Christians.

Let us do our part to prepare for their coming and training, also their going forth from us as they are sent into the fields, white for harvest. Let us prepare our fellow laborers diligently for we will share in their labor of love, as new souls are reached and equipped for Jesus Christ and the spreading of His gospel.

Chapter 13- Troubling Times Have Been Prophesied.

When the enemy shall come in like a flood, the Spirit of the Lord shall lift up a standard against him. (Isaiah 59:19b). These times are happening now, when Christians work will be very difficult in parts of the World. Today we are seeing these things coming to pass. We are seeing the systematic elimination of Christianity in many countries. Today it is very important we know what is taking place elsewhere and pray for our brethren who are being persecuted because of their worship of God. They are risking and giving their lives because of their faith. There are over 160,000 (more like 250,000) of our brethren who die each year because of their Christian faith; there are probably just as many that we do not know of. This is taking place worldwide and increasing dramatically bringing us closer to what will take place during the tribulation (Revelations 7). "Yes, and all who desire to live godly in Christ Jesus will suffer persecution." (2 Timothy 3:12). The same sufferings are experienced by your brother hood in the world." (1 Peter 5) "and they overcame him by the blood of the Lamb and the word of their testimony, and they did not love their lives to the death." (Revelations 12:11)

It is time to raise our voice and let the world know what is happening. Let us not become like, Jeremiah 5:88 "They have grown fat, they are sleek; yes, they surpass the deeds of the wicked; they do not plead the cause, of the fatherless; yet they prosper and the right of the needy they do not defend." Sometimes they do not know how to defend. Many of the estimated 250,000 Christians that lost their lives to terrorism could be alive today to carry on their work, had they only known how to protect themselves, and win the terrorist at the same time. They all needed this book, "God's Answer to the 21st Century Terrorism."

Now as we continue with this thought I want to give a few facts, concerning the various nations where the killing is most severe, and give a few illustrations. Keep in mind how the information in this book could have been used for protection and salvation then and now as we proceed to the end of this present age.

G2 bulletin - June 2, 2007, "Letusreason.org." London- a report by Britain's intelligence service m16, reveals for the first time and estimated 200 million Christians in 60 countries are now facing persecution orchestrated, in part, by Al-Qaida. This same report indicates 50,000 Christians incarcerated in work camps, in North Korea, because they refuse to submit to the views of the dictator Kim Jong Il. 40,000 are imprisoned in China. M16 calculates there are 70 million "active Christians" in China all living in a climate of fear because of their beliefs. (World net daily- from Joseph Farahs G2 Bulletin June 7, 2007.)

We need to activate, "God's Answer to 21st Century Terrorist," principles, here in the U.S.A also, for we are not immune from the terrorist. World net daily, Feb 16, 2005, the bodies of a Coptic American family from Egypt including the father, Hossam 47 years old, the wife Amal 37 years old, and daughters, Sylvia, 15 and Monica, 8 were found bound and gagged with their throats slashed, a New Jersey family from Egypt. This family had a ministry to the Coptic Christians from Egypt.

Following is a short list of countries that allow persecution of Christians:

Azerbaijan: Former Russian State

July 22, 2008 Pastor Shabanov arrested for possession of a gun. The pastor was never the owner of a gun. Police planted this device to hinder the spread of Christianity.

Belarus:

Enacted a restrictive 2002 religious law, "Only religious associations- made up of at least ten registered religious communities, including at least one active on the territory of Belarus for at least 20 years- have the right to invite foreign citizens, to conduct religious activity." On October 16, 2008 protestant Bishop Veniamin Brakh was deported from Belarus, because of his active religious activities. Forum 18 News report.

China:

Confiscation of Bibles to imprisonment, to reeducation in labor camps, to beatings and torture await those caught preaching the word in China. Pastor "Bike" Zhang and sons, C.A.A. China Aid Association. Harassment of house church Christians increased last year, a total of 2027 Christians that were affected in 2008, and 788 in 2007. Of the 2027 Christians in 2008, 764 were arrested, and 35 were sentenced to prison terms. In Beijing the total persecuted was 539, according to C.A.A.

England:

A nurse was suspended for offering to pray for one of her patients. In December of 2008 she had been warned when she offered a prayer card to another gentleman patient. The care givers informed her employer about this also. The employer called this misconduct and terminated her employment.

Eritrea:

On August 15, 2008 Eritrean authorities locked eight high school students in a metal shipping container and burned hundreds of Bibles at Sawa Defense Training Center, saying, "Sawa is a place of patriotism, not a place of pents (Pentecostals)." The Eritrean government cracks down on Christians, by placing them in metal containers, which are extremely hot during the day and cold during the night. Nearly 1800 Eritrean Christians are believed to be under arrest because of their religious beliefs, held in police stations, military camps and prisons in 12 known locations across Eritrea. It is also believed that more than 28 clergymen are being held. V.O.M. Posted August 14, 2008. Voice of the Martyrs, magazine.

Iraq:

November 12, 2008 two sisters were killed and their mother wounded by a gang of Islamic extremist in Mosul, Iraq. The gunmen shot one sister as she was waiting for a bus outside their home. They then stormed into the home, killed the other sister and injured their mother. This incident is the latest in a series of attacks on Christians that have occurred in Mosul in recent weeks. Since October, more than seven Christians have been killed and more that 200 families displaced. The Christian community in Iraq is estimated to be 3 percent of Iraq's 26 million people, or about 800,000. Some Christians believe they are being targeted in an effort to destroy, the Christian communities' economic activity and drive believers from the area. Since 2003, Christian leaders, churches and businesses in Iraq have been targeted by Islamic extremist, as a result many believers have fled. (Voice of the Martyrs, posted December 17, 2008, persecution.com)

India:

India, is one of the worst nations in the world for the way they treat Christians. Churches have been torched and Christians murdered in the waves of brutal attacks by Hindu militant in India. In Front line fellowship posted on December 24, 2008 mobs of radical Hindus attacked Christian Churches throughout the State of Orissa, burning churches, beating Christians, looting homes, schools, medical centers and clinics run by Christians. They have attacked congregations with guns, spears, axes, knives and other traditional weapons. Thousands of Christians have lost their homes, and hundreds are missing. The number of dead

Christians is not yet known. In Karnataka, India on July 13, 2008, Hindu extremists disrupted a morning service, beating the Pastor and also the Evangelist, they burned song books and Bibles. On July 19, 2008 a Christian school teacher died after being beaten by Muslim youth. VOM contacts Kerala, India. On October 10, 2008 the VOM contacts working to assist believers affected by attacks in Orissa State India, reported that more than 70,000 Christians have been displaced, and forced to live in refugee camps. "At the peyton relief camp, which houses 35 families and 130 distraught tribal's and the orphanage for 50 children in Sarongada, spent three days in the forest after their houses and churches were razed with fire. The leaders have not yet been reunited with the children. The august 2008 attacks resulted in more then 116 believers killed and more than 50,000 believers displaced. VOM Jan 14, 2009 four Christians arrested on false charges of forcible conversions in the village of Kushalpura, India, they are still in detention. V.O.M Jan 22, 2009 India Update-Christians relief camps closed in Orissa State, forcing thousands of Christians displaced by the wave of violence that began last August 2008, to flee according to V.O M contact

I am now being drawn to Revelations 2:18-29. The church at Thyatira chapter 3:1-6 the church at Sardis. Chapter 3:7-13, the Philadelphia church, and chapter 3: 14-22 the church at Laodicea.

These churches are still active today, at least their types.

The church at Thyatira is the present "Papal Church" or the Catholic Church, 500 AD until now. The Church at Sardis is referred to as the reformed church, AD 1500 until now. The Philadelphia church is the missionary Church that began about 1800 AD until now. The Church at Laodicea is referred to as the "Apostate Church," AD .1900 it is very evident in our culture today, which means the rapture is to take place very soon. The remaining Churches are Ephesus, Apostolic. Smyrna, Martyr. Pergamos, the State church. This is like China and the Old

Russian Church. We still have these churches today in various forms throughout the world.

The church of Laodicea and the church of Pergamos, are the registered State Churches in China and Russia. We also have the underground Church of Smyrna, Ephesus and Philadelphia Churches, all combined to make up the Chinese underground Church also the underground movement in other countries.

In Europe, and to a lesser degree in the USA, we find the combination of the Philadelphia Thyatira, Sardis and the church of Laodicea which is the, falling away, part of the church.

This falling away is grieving the precious Holy Spirit more than many other things, because the leaders are tired of listening, tired of praying for answers to their problems, so are using psychology and other scientific means to lure their congregations to sleep, when at the same time, "The day of the Lord" draws nearer and nearer.

The Holy Spirit want us to revive ourselves, and become white hot again, and press on for the prize that awaits us, by arresting the terrorist, and so many other haters of God. The Holy Spirit wants to show, God's power in the Church again. Even in Europe and the USA, many have left the Church because the Church seemed to be so weak and helpless, leaving the impression that the Church needed help more than the sinners we are to be reaching.

In Revelations 3:16 it states, "So because you are lukewarm and neither cold nor hot, I will spit you out of my mouth"! We are free moral agents, God will not force us to serve Him so if we are to become "Hot" for the things of God, then we must set aside special time to spend with Him, then through this fellowship restored, He will return us to our first love. We must absolutely observe Mark 12:30-31, to have this restoration completed. "And thou shall love the Lord thy God with all thy heart, and with all thy Soul, and with all thy mind, and with all thy strength; this is the first commandment. 31, And the second is like, namely this, thou shall love thy neighbor as thyself. There is none other commandment greater than these."

We now have a choice to make. In Joshua 24:15 it says "And if it seem evil unto you to serve the Lord, choose you this day whom ye will serve; ... but as for me and my house, we will serve the Lord.

As we close this chapter, I beg of you, do not be "Cold or lukewarm" towards God but believe Him, trust Him and become "Hot" for God's ways.

Becoming cold or Luke warm is a negative response. God wants a positive response. I believe with all my heart that this time in our spiritual journey can be the most magnificent, and profound as at any time since the founding of the church. Evangelism to all even the most vile and haters of God, we have a new tool now to use, let us become proficient in it's use, and make this the greatest soul winning time. Let us all endeavor to please Him with all that we are and all that we have, Praise the LORD.

Chapter 14: Enjoy These Times of Great Visitation. Be an Active Participant

This chapter begins with Revelation 3:1 the Church in Sardis. This Church is being described as a dead Church, AD 1520-AD 1750. Christianity was just coming out of the dark ages and at the end of this period Martin Luther declared "that the just should live by faith."

Following this age, came the Philadelphia Church, this is shown in Revelations 3:7. This period AD 1750-AD1900 was known as, the missionary church of brotherly love. This church enjoyed a time of great revival also this church age was blessed with great preachers, such as Wesley's, Finney, Spurgeon, DL Moody, and many others. During this same period all the missionary societies were established and the mission field opened, also great religious institutions and organizations found their birth. How different today, mission fields are closing, church doors are closing, great preachers are scarce and the Bible is rejected, why? When Jesus was talking to the apostle John in Revelations 3:8, He said "I have set before thee an open door and no man can shut it: for you have a little strength." In this verse he was still speaking to the Philadelphia Church, the missionary church and there is no mention of this door being closed by Jesus or the Holy Spirit.

We are now living in the period of the church of Laodicea. In Revelations 3:14-22 it states in verse 15, "I know thy works, that thou are neither cold nor hot: I would you were cold or hot. 16, So then because you are Luke warm, and neither cold nor hot, I will spew you out of my mouth. 17, Because you say I am rich, and increased with goods, and have need of nothing; and you do not know that you are wretched and miserable, and poor, and blind, and naked; 18, I counsel you to buy of me gold tried in the fire, that you may be rich and white garment, that you may be clothed, and that the shame of your nakedness does not appear; and anoint your eyes with eye salve, that you may see. 19, As many as I love, I rebuke and chasten; be zealous therefore, and repent. 20, Behold I stand at the door and knock, [Behold I stand outside your heart and church door knocking. Can you hear me? If so open the door.] and I will come in and sup with you, and you with me. 21, I want to make you an over comer, so that you may sit with me in my throne, even as I overcome and am sit down with my father in his throne."

Can you hear what the Holy Spirit is asking of you and your Church or fellowship? In verse 22, it says "He that has an ear let him hear what the spirit says to the churches. In Revelations 3:8 it says "I know your works: behold I have set before you an open door, and no man can shut it: for you have a little strength and have kept my word and have not denied my name." The door opened for the Philadelphia Church is still open for us today. No man can close it and the Holy Spirit hasn't closed it. Only a few men have declared various countries closed. However the word declares in Revelations 3:8 "… Behold I have set before thee an open door and no man can shut it . To claim that it is shut is a lie of Satan.

I believe with all my heart that in the Countries, where it is thought the Church has closed or closing, the closing is only to the methods used up until now. The Holy Spirit wishes a new approach to this mission project so that we may continue through the open door, which he has provided until the very end.

May we all begin using the instruction in, "God's Answer to 21st Century Terrorist" as we begin to reclaim our open door position in all the countries of the World. We win, the church is strengthened, and encouraged, and empowered.

Speaking again about the Philadelphia Church in Revelations 3:8 again it says "For you have a little strength" meaning that though feeble, their vital energy was not wholly gone. The sense is, that although they had not the highest degree of energy, or had not all that the Savior desired, they should have, they like us were not dead or cold or Luke warm. The Savior saw among them, and us, the evidence of spiritual life. There was abundant opportunity to employ all this energy and zeal which they had (little strength) and go through the open door to the World. The Philadelphia Church did not complain about the, little strength but with what they had they, through Jesus Christ, accomplished great things. The apostle Paul in 2 Corinthians 2:9 amplified Himself too weak to defeat this, messenger of Satan, so he ask Jesus about it and here is what Jesus said "My strength and power are made perfect fulfilled and complete and show themselves most effective in (your) weakness. In your weakness Paul, I can use my strength to accomplish all that needs to be accomplished but I need you to stay focused and make an effort with what you have, so that I can multiply the effectiveness of your strength and as we work together, we win." In Mark 16:20 amplified it says "And they went forth, and preached everywhere (with their little strength) the Lord working with them and confirming the word with signs following."

We are now living in the, church of Laodicea age, AD 1900-present where being Luke warm is the in thing, and the Churches are losing members, the mission offices are closing, and missionaries are coming home. Just recently, on a Christian TV station, the statement was made that only 2% of Europeans and English are still Christians. According to, 2 Thessalonians 2:1-3 there will be a falling away first and the churches will be losing members by the thousands, then the anti Christ can be revealed "Now we beseech you brethren, by the coming of our Lord Jesus Christ, and by our gathering together unto Him. 2, That you be not soon shaken in mind or be troubled, neither by spirit, nor by word, nor by letters as from us, as that the day of Christ is at hand. 3, Let no man deceive you by any means: for that day shall not come, except there come a falling away first and that man of sin be revealed, the son of perdition."

Now dear reader and Christian friends, I want to offer you, as well as me, a challenge. We are living in the last days before Jesus returns for us. Does Revelations 3:15-17 identify you and me? Are we dead, cold and Luke warm in our Christian experience? No, absolutely not me and hopefully not you, as well. Then what must we do to rekindle the little strength in us for God's glory?

We must begin to pray, fast and recommit our lives to Jesus. We must be totally sold out to Jesus and focus on Him. I am a" Hot "Christian, Revelations 3:15-17 does not identify me. I am an exception. I have every intention to be the strongest and best I can possibly be for my Lord. There are no closed countries; there are no closed doors, there is not a situation too bad for God and me.

I, 100% agree with Jesus in Matthew 18:11 "For the Son of man is come to save that which was lost." He, Jesus and I, are seeking the lost all over the world, my little strength and His perfect strength will find the Paul's, Peter's, Stephen's, and Phillip's out there hiding from me. I intend to find these haters of God, these terrorist, and see the Holy Spirit bring them into the kingdom of God through Him working with me. Then when we are white hot for souls, we can be numbered in Matthew 20:1-16 the parable of the laborers. We are working last and are more excited and joyous than even those who have gone before us. Let us make these last days a time of a greater receiving of souls, than ever before, for Jesus will be working with us.

Conclusion

Let us analyze our picture of Jesus and Paul, Saul the 1st century terrorist.

1. An invisible, Holy Spirit, fence or shield around Damascus so that Saul cannot enter.
2. As Saul approached this barrier he saw a bright light "Jesus arrived".
3. Saul was blinded and fell to the ground, not blinded by the light but by the gift of blindness given to the church. 2 Kings 6. Elisha, etc. (chains and ropes dropped).
4. Jesus identified Himself as the cause of Saul's dilemma, problem.
5. Saul now responds to the truth, his ears and heart have received the word of God directly. Who are you? Then, what will you have me to do?
6. Instruction to go for further teaching and fellowship, now into Damascus.
7. Saul followed the instruction and was for 3 days, praying and fasting, while still blind.
8. Ananias arrived and lay hands on Saul and his sight was restored, Saul was then baptized, In the Holy Spirit.
9. Paul was, reluctantly, received into the church, for fellowship and personal growth.
10. Paul then begun to preach Jesus, as Lord and Savior, and the forgiver of sin.

Step by Step

1. Holy Spirit Fence:

    a. About 5 ft. in diameter, around children, parents, pastors all church members. At least 100 ft. from all churches, outbuildings, schools, homes and all meeting places. Do not forget the new converts, cover them also.

    b. When the haters of Jesus have been arrested, do not be afraid of them, remember the, Jesus picture, of Paul being arrested and blinded. Go to them, they need you to comfort them, as to what is happening to them and why.

2. Identify the blindness with Jesus.

    a. Some have never heard of Jesus, so ask them first, have you heard of Him? According to their answer, begin there, to tell about Jesus, the love He has for them, and their great need for Him. What He has done to save them and prepare them for Heaven. The way they were going, they were doomed to hell. In His mercy He wants to welcome them home to Himself and to His Father. When they receive Him, He heals them of blindness.

3. Personal care needed, now.

    a. They will need time for instruction in the ways of Jesus. They may need a place to stay during this time. Again, do not be afraid, because the fire of hate has been quenched by Jesus Christ, now they need your love and care. Take care of every need of the blind man or woman. They are your new brother or sister so give them a good impression of their new found freedom in Jesus.

b. They may be taken into your church, home or some other convenient place, here they can be taught and fed for 3-4 days, as was the apostle Paul. They may or may not want food and they may have a hard time sleeping. Remember they have been arrested when they were at the highest level of hatred and blindness has totally removed the hate they are now so very tender so love them, help then recover and enjoy the beginning of their new life.

4. 3-4 days after the arrest and instruction.

a. They need a time with the elders of the church. The elders should listen to their testimony and determine how much they have learned and where more training and teaching can take place.

b. At this time also there should be a baptismal service, where these new converts can be baptized and receive their new sight for their new journey and life with Jesus Christ. At this time they may already know where they must go and whom they must see to deliver the first gospel message to come out of a new, clean heart and mouth.

5. Not all the conversions are the same.

a. The preparations you have made to win the terrorist may not be like the Paul conversion picture. Every one will prepare the area differently but the results will be the same. Please feel free to adapt your surroundings with the facilities available to you. The basic preparations, like the Holy Spirit fence, must be placed first. Please do not forget the Holy Spirit wants to work with us so we all can become soul winners.

b. Now that you know how to protect yourself and your loved ones, do it. Don't wait another minute. Just walk around your home, church or apartment. Don't have an accident where we are destroyed because of laziness. Just do it and get ready for your harvest. Let the terrorist come, we are ready for them. Praise God!

The Author

The author has endured many agonizing hours of hearing about and watching the innocent people of the world, brutalized by tyrants and powerful people who do not seem to care about those entrusted to them. Very recently this author received a new perspective of the persecuting situation. Now through love we have the opportunity to see many terrorist changed.

About the Book

"God's Answer to the 21st Century Terrorist" is a memorable account of a fresh historical perspective with unforgettable characters and with a touch of the supernatural.

The apostle Paul was a 1st century terrorist, killing and imprisoning Christians. The Lord Jesus Christ, Head of the Church, gave us an object lesson in how to win the terrorist. We need to use His plan today. Too many Christians are being slaughtered, the churches burned and whole congregations being threatened with violence.

Key Words

Terrorist, Blindness, Holy Spirit, Innocent, Churches, Burning, Injustice, Imprison, Christians, Beheading, Salvation, Conversion.

References

To Frontline Fellowship:

Permission to reproduce: those wishing to reprint or quote from any edition of Frontline   Fellowship News are encouraged to do so. Provided that it is quoted in context and that due acknowledgement of source is given. Please send a copy of any article to us. E-mail, admin@frontline.org.

To Compass Direct News:

Material on this site may be shared by an individual or bloggers, with credit to Compass Direct news. www.compassdirect.org.

To Mr. Jim Jacobson, president of Christian Freedom International and their news letters which keep me informed about persecuted Christians around the World. Info@ Christianfreedom.org. 1-800-323-2273

To Mr. Tom White, director of the Voice of The Martyrs monthly publication and the weekly news letters, another special source of information about the persecuted Christians around the World. www.Persecution.com 1-877-337-0302.

Scriptures noted AMP is taken from the Amplified Bible. Copyright c 1954, 1962, 1965, 1987 by, The Lockman Foundation, used by permission.

Scriptures noted NKJV are taken from the New King James Version. Copyright c 1979, 1980, 1982 by, Thomas Nelson, Inc publishers.

Dedication

This book is dedicated to all the Christian martyrs from ages past until the very present. Your sacrifice has not been in vain. From this day forward we expect to be reaching and convincing, more and more of the persecutors, to follow Jesus Christ, Our Savior, and Head of the Church, and Our God.

Acknowledgments

To my dearest friend Yong Griffee, who kept prodding me to finish the book and who worked so tirelessly to allow me time to write. Then to Yong Grifffee's daughter, Cheryl, for taking the time from Snow boarding to type the original manuscript. Then to all my other family members and friends, for their encouragement and support.